Giving Up

Giving Up

The Last Days of Sylvia Plath

Jillian Becker

St. Martin's Press ❧ New York

www.stmartins.com

ISBN 0-312-31598-8

First published in Great Britain by Ferrington, Bookseller & Publisher

First U.S. Edition: May 2003

10 9 8 7 6 5 4 3 2 1

Giving Up

1

The Last Days

If events in a writer's life are worth recording, they should have the virtue of having happened; so I'd better set down my memories of Sylvia Plath while I still have them. I gave some to biographers, but they suppressed the information or distorted it, not only with inaccuracies but also by tailoring it to make a point.

I met her after she and her husband, Ted

Hughes, had parted. We quickly became friends but only for the last few months of her life. She was lonely, almost friendless as well as husbandless. The flattering courtiers had departed with the king.

On a freezing Thursday in February 1963 at about two in the afternoon she called me from a pay phone (she had no phone in her apartment) and said only, "May I come round with the children?" Half an hour later she arrived at my house on Mountfort Crescent, an ear off Barnsbury Square in Islington.

One of her erstwhile friends was sitting in my study. On seeing her, Sylvia stopped in the doorway, did not greet her or return her smile but turned abruptly to me and asked if she could go and lie down. I led her upstairs to a bedroom. "I feel terrible," she said. The children played with my youngest daughter, Madeleine, who was about the same age as Nick. My other visitor remembered she had to be somewhere and hurried off.

At about four Sylvia came down and told me that she would "rather not go home." She gave me the keys to her apartment and asked me to fetch toothbrushes, nightclothes and such; also a "posh" dress, blue with silver thread, and a bag of hair-setting rollers; and two books: a novel called *The Ha-Ha* by Jennifer Dawson and *Escape from Freedom* by Erich Fromm.

She had taken a lease on the upper two floors of a house on Fitzroy Road, where the poet W. B. Yeats had lived for a while. There was a blue plaque on its façade commemorating his stay. To Sylvia, the association of the place with him was its chief attraction. Its location was pleasant, Fitzroy Road off Regent's Park Road, which was lined from end to end—Chalcot Crescent to Gloucester Crescent—with the pads of persons soon to be famous in the arts, television, films, academia, journalism, music, opera, theater, satire, photography—and, for all I know, pop, sport and fashion too: a string of luminaries about to be switched on. When the satirical magazine *Private Eye* was started as one of the blooms of that efflorescence, it carried a cartoon serial called "N.W.1" after the postal district of the road and its offshoots. More wittily than wickedly, it satirized the manners and morals of fashionable-intellectual London, soon to amplify into "swinging London."

The Yeats house had once been quite spacious, but its conversion into a two-dwelling building, with a flat on the ground floor and the "duplex" apartment above, had made it rather cramped. The way into Sylvia's sitting room was through the darkish kitchen in which one of those small three or four-ringed gas cookers, with a grill or plate rack hanging over the hob, stood in one corner. The sitting room was the only room of a decent size. It was bright. Its two sash windows, with curtains of red corduroy, overlooked Fitzroy Road. The furnishing was sparse; just a couple of chairs, a bookcase and a rug on the floor, as best I can remember.

On my first visit Sylvia had told me, "I want Americans to rent this place in the summer, so I must get a sofa. Americans always want a sofa." From a narrow wall-shelf I picked up a small puritan-plain wooden box with POOR BOX painted on it and a slot for coins in its lid. She could have been displaying it as a charming antique; she might have put it there as a reproach to Hughes; or perhaps she hoped it would do what it was made for—collect small change. It was empty. She said, "Oh, that was a present. It used to belong in the church near Court Green" (the property in Devon which she and Hughes had bought).

I hadn't seen the upper floor of her apartment until the afternoon I fetched her things. Immediately to the left at the top of the stairs was a door with a sign hung on it: QUIET! GENIUS AT WORK! It opened into her tiny workroom. There was a small table and a chair in it, and as far as I can remember nothing else and no space for anything else. The table was her writing desk. It was tidy, with very little on it: paper, pens in a jar, and one of the books she'd asked for.

I found everything she wanted for herself, and the pile of stuff for Nick that babies always travel heavy with, but no change of clothes at all for the little girl; none in the chest of drawers in the children's room, none with the laundry, none, except only a nightdress or pajamas, I forget which. As I had three daughters of my own, my house contained a plethora of girls' clothes in various sizes; not Frieda's size, but adaptable. I could also wash her things overnight. And I could take her shopping, which is what I did a few days later, after her mother's death.

I bathed and fed Frieda and Nick with Madeleine. (My two older girls went off early for a weekend with their father and stepmother in St. John's Wood, to make space for our visitors.) When all the children were settled for the night I heated chicken soup, grilled large rump steaks, and made mashed potatoes with plenty of milk and butter, and a salad, then fetched Sylvia to join me in the dining room. The walls were striped with red and gold, and on one of them, "holding the stripes down," hung a dozen prints of the original drawings for the Gibson Girl cartoons in *Punch* magazine. We'd inherited them from the previous owner of the house. On her first visit to us, Sylvia had read all the captions but hadn't smiled.

She ate heartily. She always did and it always pleased me; not only because it was a compliment to my cooking but chiefly because eating well was bound to make her feel better. Like most Jewish mothers, I believed in the therapeutic power of good food, especially chicken soup. But actually, my husband Gerry was more the earth-mother type than I was, and it crossed my mind that Sylvia might have been looking for consolation from him rather than from me. But he was in bed with the flu—hence the chicken soup made earlier. He didn't feel well enough to come down to dinner on that first night of her stay.

Sylvia talked bitterly about her husband and Assia Wevill, the woman he was living with. She asked me why I thought Assia's husband, David, had been so passive about his wife's leaving him for another man. I told her I couldn't make either of them out, had never got more than an impression of them. They'd come to parties at our house a few times, and once we gave them dinner when they turned up uninvited— having mistaken the date of an invitation. They were both rather costive conversationalists. Assia seemed to have nothing much to say. Wevill might have had some interesting ideas, but he spoke so softly that I found it hard to hear him, and never felt it worthwhile to per- severe with a bent neck and strained attention. I repeated to her something I'd been told (by the woman who'd been in my study when Sylvia had arrived—an imaginative person, quite an artist with gossip). The story was that when Assia had announced to Wevill that she was leaving him and why, he had punched his fist through the glass panel of a door. "That was all he did?" Sylvia asked, slightly shaking her head to imply *No help from that quarter, then.*

She went to bed early, and asked me to sit beside her. She showed me two bottles of pills and told me she must take two of one sort at ten o'clock and two of the other between six and eight in the morning, depending on when she woke. I set a jug of water and a tumbler on the bedside table, and at about ten interrupted our talk to remind her to take the night pills. They didn't seem to make her somnolent or even soothe her. She talked on, about people I didn't know as if they had been part of my life too. In the same musing tone she said, "It would be good to get the children away to the seaside. Somewhere warm. They haven't been well. I wish I could take them to Spain. Ted took *her* to Spain, did you know that?"

"If I didn't have the older children to look after in the middle of a school term, I would take you," I said. "Perhaps when the Easter holidays come I could rent a place in Spain. Or Italy. I prefer Italy."

"Easter—that's a long way off," she said.

She talked about Court Green. It was "not easy to keep;" there were "acres of linoleum" which needed polishing. She had a "cleaning lady," but still felt overburdened with chores, especially when the children weren't well. There was a girl here in London who'd promised to come and live in as an "au pair" and help with the children, the shopping and cooking and laundry, but had changed her mind, and now the difficult hunt for someone suitable would have to start all over again. When she and Ted, she said, had moved to Court Green, they'd thought their ideal life was starting. The country was Ted's natural habitat. And hers. When the Wevills had come down to visit them there on "that fatal day," Assia had so obviously not belonged in the country. Sylvia had watched with scorn while "Mrs. Wevill" had picked her way, teetering in her high-heeled shoes, among the cowpats in the slushy fields. "It's strange that she wore high heels in the country," I said, "because in town I saw her always in flat shoes." But she repeated the story, and I accepted the high heels. They conveyed so aptly what Assia was, or seemed, both to Sylvia and me: vain and shallow.

I recounted to Sylvia an incident that took place at a party of ours in the spring or early summer of 1962, before she and I had met. Assia had asked if she could listen to a radio "somewhere quiet." I took her to my study, found the program she wanted on the radiogram—Ted Hughes and Sylvia Plath reading their poetry—and left her alone with it. Sylvia nodded slowly as I told her this, as if to say *Yes, that figures.*

She dozed off at last and I went wearily to our four-poster bed in which Gerry lay, restless and snoring. An hour or two later Nick cried and woke Frieda. I took them both to Sylvia and fetched a warmed bottle of milk for Nick. When we'd gotten them back to sleep, she returned to her bed and I thankfully to mine. But after another hour or so I heard her calling me. She couldn't sleep, she said. "This is always the worst time, this hour of the morning. I wonder if I could take another pill?"

"Not if it's not prescribed," I said, accepting the role of nurse. "If you're wakeful," I suggested, "you could read for a while." Fromm and *The Ha-Ha* lay beside her.

"I'm not quite wakeful enough to read," she said. "Is it nearly morning?"

It was not yet three.

"Too early to take my waking-up pills then?"

"Much too early."

I sat on a low Victorian "grandmother chair," with the bedside lamp switched off and only the light from the landing coming into the room. As my eyes grew used to the dimness I could see that her eyes were closed. But she was still restless. When her breathing told me she was asleep, I went back to my room.

In the morning, after she'd taken her pills and devoured a good breakfast, she phoned the young woman who had reneged on her promise to come to her as an "au pair." Sylvia pleaded with her to keep her promise, but she wouldn't. Then Sylvia had a long talk with her doctor. I knew him—John Horder—both as the father of my daughter Claire's best friend at school, and as a partner in the medical practice with which we had been registered when we too had lived in the neighborhood of Regent's Park Road. He asked to speak to me.

"How does she seem to you?"

"Depressed. She finds it hard to get to sleep at night."

"Did she take her pills?"

"Yes, and they worked eventually."

"She must take her pills night and morning. Will you see that she does? But don't do everything for her. She must look after the children. She must feel that she's absolutely necessary to them."

I understood why that was important. I said I'd try to get her to feed them and bathe them and play with them, and from then on I'd ask her to come with me when I took them to the bathroom, the changing table, the kitchen, the toy-cupboard. I'd wait for her to pick up a spoon, a sponge or whatever, but she didn't. I'd leave the room, but she'd follow me or wait for my return. I had to choose between letting them go hungry and unwashed until she attended to them, or do what needed to be done. Most of the time, I eventually did it. Once when Nick needed to be changed and washed and dried after he'd defecated, she watched absently for a while, then put her hands on my shoulders to move me aside, saying "Now that's really beyond the call of duty. Let me do it." And I would have let her, but the job was done.

On Saturday evening Sylvia put on or packed

seen, whatever had been said, had resolved something for her, I thought. We lingered at the table, as we usually did, for an hour or so after the coffee cups had gone cold, talking about something that has left not a trace of a memory. The children fell asleep, and the wine we had drunk made us sleepy too so we all went to lie down. At teatime Sylvia told us she'd slept deeply. She ate and drank and talked, the children played contentedly. Nothing in particular was said or done to change the easy mood we all seemed to share, when Sylvia got up briskly and began gathering things and putting them into carrier bags. She declared she "must get home tonight." Had she only just remembered something that needed doing? What energized her, made her so suddenly purposeful? Was it a decision to change her life—or (I wonder with hindsight) to die? Can a decision to die flush one through with a sense of excitement and urgency? Or was the bustle of commitment a deceptive performance, concealing a plunge into deepest despair? If so, it was an amazingly successful effort of will. She seemed invigorated, mildly elated, as I'd seldom if ever seen her before.

She asked Gerry to drive them home. "Of course I will," he said, "if you want me to. But do you really have to go?"

She had things to do, she said, so many things, all of them urgent.

"I must get Frieda to school. A nurse will be looking in early. She started coming when the children were ill and I want her to see that Nick is really well now. And I must sort the laundry."

I knew that there was very little laundry to sort.

"You will remember to take your pills?" I said, playing the nurse's part, though she didn't seem just then to need an overseer. On the contrary, she seemed thoroughly in charge of herself. And busy with the packing, she didn't answer.

"Sylvia?" I said. Her eyes met mine. She

wanted me to believe her. "Yes, I'll remember," she said.

Everything was all right then. In fact, her decision to go solved a small difficulty for me. On and off over the weekend I had been considering how to accommodate everyone when my two older daughters came home. Sylvia had Claire's room, Frieda and Nick were in Lucy's. There were bedrooms and a bathroom at the top of the house, narrowed by the slope of the roof but not uncomfortable. I could, I thought, move Sylvia and her children up there so that Claire and Lucy could have their own rooms; or I could move their clothes and books upstairs and let Sylvia and the little people stay where they were, across the landing from me, where I could reach them quickly and easily.

But there was something else, another reason why I felt a sense of relief when she insisted on going home; a heavier reason, not to be thought about or discussed as frankly and easily as the practical question of room arrangements. The truth was she had tired me. Her need for my attention had begun to seem relentless. I doubted I could carry on much longer as I had for those few days and nights. But as long as she was in my house, whenever she implored me to stay beside her and listen to her, or whenever her children needed attention and didn't get it from her, I would have to do what was necessary. When they got home their needs would no longer be my responsibility. I would not have to fear the moment when her distraught unhappiness welled up in her again—and it would, I knew, however firmly in charge of herself she might be for an hour or two.

She wanted to go, and nothing I could have done or said would have kept her against her will. And then there was Dr. Horder's injunction: "She must look after the children, feel she's necessary to them."

I stood in the open door or under the portico to see them off. It was very cold. The snow lay thick on everything, whitening Gerry's black car, an old meterless London taxicab. Gerry, wearing a donkey jacket and fur hat, helped them into the back, put the bags at their feet and shut them in. Soon warm air would waft through to them from the front cabin where the driver sat alone. He tied on the butcher's apron he always wore for driving, to protect his clothes from the grease that dripped from an undiscovered egress on the shaft of the steering wheel, climbed into his seat, slammed the door and started the engine. I raised my hand, she raised hers, off they went, and I hurried indoors. For the moment I felt more relief than worry. But when Gerry came back and told me that she had wept on the way home, worry came tinged with guilt.

He habitually left the sliding glass window between the front and back of the old cab open so he could talk to passengers and hear what they said if they shouted. The vehicle rattled and roared, and it was only when he stopped at a traffic light that he heard her sobbing. He pulled over, got out, and went to sit with her in the back. Her head was in her hands. Perched on a jump seat facing them, he held her shoulders. Then the children began to cry too, and he had to take them on his knees. "Sylvia, let me take you back home with me. Jillian doesn't want you to go. I don't want you to go. Come back," he urged her. But she lifted her head and said, "No, this is nonsense, take no notice. I have to get home."

He wasn't easily reassured. He told me he asked her many times, "Are you sure?" and she answered as often as he asked that she was absolutely sure. So he drove on and saw her into her apartment with the children and the bags. I pictured him embracing her in his usual bear hug, saying a few words to the children and kissing them good night.

"I promised her," he told me, "that I'll look in tomorrow on my way home. And I told her if she wants to come back here she should just drive over."

"Did she say she would?" By then I was more than half hoping she'd given him an assurance that she would come back.

"She said she'd be fine."

"She didn't say she'd come back tomorrow?"

"No."

"But you think she may come?"

"She knows she can if she wants to."

With that I had to be satisfied. I slept soundly that night, and was up and dressed and had given the children their breakfast when the phone rang at about half past eight. It was Dr. Horder to tell me that Sylvia had killed herself.

She had done it at the time when she always felt worst, just before day began with its noises and duties and human contacts and small consolations. She had not taken her morning pills. Instead, she had given up living.

Dr. Horder told me how she'd done it, gassing herself in her kitchen oven. About an hour earlier the nurse had found her, and a note saying he was to be called. How could he get hold of her husband, he asked me, to tell him that his wife was dead and his children in need of him? I had to find out from others.

Later Hughes phoned me, and in the evening Gerry and I went to Fitzroy Road to meet him. He talked to Gerry about the children. He asked us nothing about Sylvia in her last days—not then. Later in the week, when Sylvia's brother Warren and his wife Margaret had flown over from America and moved into the apartment with the children, releasing Hughes to go back to wherever it was he was living with Assia Wevill, he took to phoning me in the small hours of the morning. Self-absorbed as he was, he would wake me at the ebb-tide of the blood-sugar when the mind is least reliable, just as his wife had done, to ask the questions that arose to trouble him. What had she said? What had she done? I answered when I could, but he didn't really listen to my answers. Once he sounded hostile, accusing ("Did you say you thought the children should be taken care of from now on by Warren and Margaret?"). I had not, but I barely had time to deny it before he'd gone on to something else. It couldn't have been the reason for his call. After all, how could it matter what I thought about the arrangements he made for his children? And even if he'd been willing to hear me speak, what could I (what could anyone) have said to save him from the furies of his own darkest hours?

2

Remembered Conversations

In those last days and nights, she talked mostly about how she felt, what she wanted, what she remembered, what should have and might have happened, and how nothing could repair what had been broken, nothing restore what had been lost. She said often, "I feel terrible." She said it when I took her upstairs to lie down just after she'd arrived, and again in the night and the next day, not only when she was alone with me, but also when the children were there, and when Gerry joined us in the study on her second evening with us. Still feeling unwell, he put music on the gramophone to console himself and her. Later he and I had to go out for an hour or two, so we left an ex-student of Gerry's (Gerry was a lecturer in English) to keep Sylvia company, and help, if necessary, with the children if they woke. Before we left, the young man held out his pack of cigarettes to her and me. I shook my head. "I've given up," I said.

"Oh, why give anything up?" said Sylvia, who was soon to give up everything.

At her request, the young man put on longplaying records of Beethoven, Bach, Gluck, Purcell, Vivaldi. She said she had only quite recently "discovered" music; that we had "given it to her." On our return, as we entered the house, we could hear "I have lost my Eurydice," sung by—I think—Janet Baker. It was painfully beautiful.

In the months before those last days of her life I had seen her quite often. There was a festival of some filmmaker's work at the Everyman Cinema in Hampstead, and once a week I took her to see one of his films. They were comedies but they didn't make her laugh. I cannot remember Sylvia laughing, though I know from her work, in particular her novel *The Bell Jar,* that she had a sense of humor. ("He just stood there in front of me [naked] and I kept on staring at him. The only thing I could think of was turkey neck and turkey gizzards. . . .") In all probability she didn't see the film she was watching. "Shall we go to the next one, or have you had enough?" I asked her after our second or third jaunt. "We must see them all," she said, so we did. Or at least I did, with her sitting next to me.

I took her to a play in the West End—I've long forgotten what it was—and afterward we sat for ages in a "caff" in Soho, the sort that stayed open all night for cab drivers. Perched on high, uncomfortable stools and leaning on the scratched Formica counter, we drank coffee and argued about psychoanalysis, she to some extent for and I wholly against it. She didn't talk about it in connection with her own "problems," but as an idea. It has hardly ever been said but should be remembered that Sylvia was an intellectual (a "no-no word" nowadays). She could hardly have won the "straight As" she was so proud of had she not been capable of rational thought—though she was hardly ever in a mood for it in 1962.

We had some things in common. We were born in the same year, 1932. We both grew up in the New World, thousands of miles from the battlefields of the Second World War, she in America, I in South Africa. We were raised on the same fictions of literature and versions of history, lived in the same language, were affected by the same distant events in different ways; developed much the same, though not identical, tastes and ambitions. We both wrote poetry, she extraordinarily well and I seldom well enough. When I read her poems for the first time—late at night, cover to cover in a copy of *Colossus* that she gave me—I suffered a bereavement: one of my most cherished hopes, that I might become a poet, quietly died. I could write verse—had even composed some lines in a dream that had still seemed good in the morning—but realized that night that I was not and would not be a poet. Did I envy Sylvia her gift? Yes, deeply, but I didn't grudge it.

Of course there were more differences between us than similarities, as there are between any two people. To name one that I will return to later, she was of Austrian-German and I of Jewish descent, and in our time that was not something that could remain of no consequence.

Sometimes we mentioned our mothers, each of us unforgivingly. In her case a need to impress her mother had been a driving force. She'd had to present her with success after success. The breakup of her marriage, she believed, was surely seen by her mother as a failure; and even though Aurelia Plath voiced no such judgment, the thought of it infuriated Sylvia. She hated the shame it would require her to feel. To shut it out she would now deny her mother any part in her life. Furthermore, she knew that Aurelia would compare her daughter's plight to her own, and it was bad enough to bear without that. "I'll be a single woman bringing up two children all by myself like my mother," she lamented to both Gerry and me a number of times.

We talked about children. She had wanted, she said, to have six. The experience of giving birth was "uniquely, incomparably wonderful."

Once she told me about a young woman she knew in Devon who was ostracized by the church-going ladies because she'd had an illegitimate child (or had sinned in some such way). Sylvia was indignant on behalf of the sinner.

She said she liked people who could teach her something—such as how to keep bees. But my impression was, and has remained, that she liked the vocabulary and images of beekeeping more than the bees themselves.

One day she asked me why people on seeing her written name pronounced it to rhyme with math.

"Why, how do you pronounce it?" I asked.

"Plaath," she said, and indeed I'd heard her say Plaath often enough.

After that reminder, I introduced her and spoke of her as Sylvia Plaath, until her name became famous as the math-rhyming Plath. But I have wondered how she came to Plaath. An American pronunciation of P-L-A-T-H is likely to keep the A short. And if it was the original German she was thinking of, then it would be closer to Plaat.

Once, early on in that long white winter, she told me about a short story she had just read and admired, praising it by saying, "It's very *worked*." If spontaneity was by then a virtue of poetry in her judgment, it was not necessarily so for composing prose.

She wasn't happy with the reviews of *The Bell Jar*. She said, "It took so long to come out I'd almost forgotten about it." I asked her why she'd published it under the name Victoria Lucas. "I didn't want the critics to judge it as the work of a poet," she said. I asked her how long it had taken to write, whether she'd found it easy or difficult. She said, not quite answering me, "When I decided to write a novel I thought something must happen, and it must happen over twenty chapters."

She told me stories about poets she'd met, their carping relations with one another, giving me an idea for a new collective noun—"a pettiness of poets." It didn't amuse her. It stung her. "Poets are no pettier than anybody else," she rebuked me.

There was one other occasion—only one other, I'm fairly sure—when something I said annoyed her. I told her that I liked a certain poem by a contemporary American woman poet. I knew it by heart and repeated it to her.

She listened, but when I'd finished she made no comment. After a few moments I said, self-defensively, that I thought it was "a perfect poem." "There can't *be* such a thing," she protested. I suspected she was a little irritated because the poem was too good rather than not good enough, but perhaps unjustly. Once when I declared a certain young poet's work to be better than somebody else's, she said, "It's not a competition."

One of the poets we shared enthusiasm for was Wallace Stevens. Reading her book *Colossus* I couldn't fail to notice his influence on her, most plainly in the poem *Snakecharmer*, but I said nothing about that; poets learn from poets; there was no need to say so. Among other Americans she mentioned were Robert Lowell and Anne Sexton, neither of whom I much liked. We both liked Robert Graves, and she told me that a young woman she knew had visited him in Majorca, and that he'd gotten her to come every day to read his poems aloud to him. I now know there were two poets she'd seen much of whose names I never heard her speak: Richard Murphy and W. S. Merwin. They belonged in her husband's world, no longer hers. (It was many years later that I read Merwin's poetry and saw that he'd had some effect on her.)

Gerry and I usually saw her separately, unless she came to our house. He would call at her place now and then on the way back from his college to see if there was anything she needed help with. When her car—a half-timbered Morris station wagon—was giving trouble, he took it to be fixed by his pet mechanic, "Big Jim." Gerry told me she talked mostly about Hughes. He reported to me once: "Sylvia says that she and Hughes made love like giants." I laughed. I don't know whether Sylvia really did say it—though I think it possible that she did—or whether it was just Gerry's version of whatever she had said.

Perhaps she had been expressing her reaction to a piece of gossip that was going the rounds. It was about Hughes taking Assia for their first lovemaking to the Ritz Hotel. As soon as they were locked in the room with peaches and champagne he had hung the DO NOT DISTURB sign on the door and told her they would be staying there for two days. The rest of the story was graphically narrated to us, but I'll cut to the bottom line. She was, it was said, "terrified of him."

I know that this had reached Sylvia because she lamented to me that his need to sin in such luxurious settings—The Ritz, the shores of the Mediterranean—so depleted their joint bank account that she and Frieda had to "survive on little more than spaghetti;" yet when, on a visit to the children, he'd found a bottle of cheap sherry in her sitting room, he'd stormed at her, "so this is what you spend my hard-earned money on?"

"He turned up in stove-pipe pants and winkle-picker shoes," she said with scorn. "That's what Mrs. Wevill's taught him—how to look fashionable." Assia worked in advertising, and fashion—Sylvia and I agreed—was "probably just about all she understood."

One evening we were sitting together over tea and scones in our dining room, whose long windows looked out on the garden. As the day faded, the setting sun gleamed out from the snow-clouds for a few moments over the white heaps of the borders, dramatically underlit the bare branches of a huge chestnut tree, and then, almost suddenly, was gone, leaving only a grayness, like dry concrete. I quoted Louis Mac-Neice: *"The sunlight on the garden hardens and grows cold/you cannot cage the minute within its nets of gold."* She said she'd "forgotten about that poem" and was glad to be reminded of it. I said I liked the rhymes in the middle of the lines and she said she did too. We became pensive. I let the dark grow round us in the room until everything except the silver teapot was indistinct, and then switched on the lights. I think she remembered that evening when she wrote *Edge: [A]s petals / Of a rose close when the gar-*

den / Stiffens—But of course I may be wrong. She had used rhymes in the middle of lines before. But it was certainly written very late in her life, possibly last of all, indicating that not all her latest poems were of the spontaneous kind, uttered rather than "worked," to be spoken aloud rather than read. *Edge* is as worked as any of the earlier poems. The meaning is terrifying. It suggests that she was thinking of killing her children when she killed herself, to avenge herself, Medea-like, on her husband. *Each dead child coiled, a white serpent, / One at each little / Pitcher of milk, now empty, / She has folded / Them back into her body* . . . (Medea had been in Sylvia's thoughts for some time: *Aftermath*, a poem in *Colossus*, refers to her "austere" tragedy.)

When the time came to make the final decision about who was to die, she set out milk for the children, but killed only herself. To kill them was, after all, only "the illusion of a Greek necessity". Believing, as most of us did, that the town gas which flowed through domestic pipes at that time would rise, lighter than air, she opened the windows of their bedroom on the floor above. (It was also an illusion of a scientific necessity, for in fact the gas sank, putting two men in the flat below into a semi-coma from which they might have lapsed further into death had the gas not been turned off before too much of it could seep through the floor.) It was one of the coldest winters of the century. Frieda and Nick might have perished from the cold had not the nurse arrived soon enough to save them. Sylvia knew she was coming—she had told me she was. But how, I wonder, did she imagine the nurse would get into the house? It was only by chance that house-painters arrived with keys on that Monday morning.

Was Sylvia giving Fate an opportunity? She had left a set of keys in my house, in the coat she'd hung on the crowded rack in my hall, but I didn't discover it until Hughes asked me some days later to look for it. "How the devil did she get into the flat?" he asked when he found the keys in the pocket. She'd had others, with which she'd unlocked the door to lead Frieda and Gerry upstairs, Gerry carrying Nick.

Had she supposed that Gerry or I would come after her during the night with her coat and keys? No. She had not expected or wanted to be saved at the last moment from self-inflicted death as she had been once before. According to Mr. Goodchild—a police officer attached to the coroner's office, who personally brought me the autopsy report on Sylvia years later when I requested it—she had thrust her head far into the gas oven. "She had really meant to die," said Mr. Goodchild. She'd blocked the cracks at the bottom of the doors to the landing and the sitting room, turned all the gas taps full on, neatly folded a kitchen cloth and placed it on the floor of the oven, and laid her cheek on it.

"Believe me," Mr. Goodchild said most earnestly, "it's just as well that no one came and pulled her out. After so many minutes of breathing in the gas [he told me exactly how many, but I have forgotten—I only remember that it was a chillingly precise number] even if your life is saved it's not worth living. Your mind is gone forever. You're a vegetable."

He told me too that the gas makes the blood bright pink. (The color of the painted hearts and roses and bright balloons that appear now and then in her poetry, incongruous among recurring images of blackness, baldness, cold hooded bony moons, beasts and birds of prey, blind white eyes, gaping crimson mouths, wounds and blood.)

When Assia Wevill killed herself, she also killed her daughter Shura, Hughes's child. Sylvia almost certainly intended to hurt Hughes with her desperate death, but when the moment came she did not commit murder. Assia did.

3

The Funeral

Sylvia had pictured her grave in undulating Devon, not flinty Yorkshire where she lies. Soon after we met she told me, speaking of her death as a far-off event, that she'd like to be buried in the churchyard next to Court Green. Had she never said as much to Hughes? I suppose if he'd held the funeral down there, none of his family would have come to it.

Gerry and I took a train to Yorkshire from London on the morning of her funeral. A journey of many hours through snow under a dismal sky. I had never travelled so far north in these islands. Passing through industrial towns, I glimpsed factories with furnaces visible through open doors, reviving images in Victorian novels I'd read as a schoolgirl, never-to-be-forgotten descriptions of women chain-smiths stripped to the waist and glistening with sweat. It was a little disappointing to see only men.

A young woman, a cousin of Hughes, met us at Hebden Bridge station and drove us up the steep road to the hilltop village of Hepstonstall. Over tea and sandwiches in his parents' house, his mother, an imposing—I would even say domineering—presence, questioned me about my friendship with Sylvia. How long had I known her? How had she seemed to me in her last days? "We all loved her, you know," she asserted—laid it down, like a law. His father didn't say much. A slight man, thin, in my memory.

The service in the church was short. For a few moments sunlight came through a stained-glass window, enriching the yellow in it.

We followed her coffin to the grave, a yellow trench in the snow, its banked-up mud the same color as the stained glass, but thick as oil paint freshly poured out. Beside it the rite was completed.

"I'll stay here alone for a while," Hughes said.

The rest of us went to the gate. I looked back and saw him standing there, a solitary figure at the foot of the grave.

He rejoined the funeral guests soon after we were seated, fourteen or so in all, round a table in a private upper room of a pub in the village. Gerry and I sat opposite each other at one end, Hughes between us.

Only four of us were there "for Sylvia:" Warren and Margaret, Gerry and I. The rest were there "for Ted," his—mostly elderly—relations. His mother had stayed at home.

Gerry bought a bottle of whisky. He and Hughes drank it silently. When the tea had been poured and steak-and-kidney pies set down at each place, Hughes blurted out vehemently but quietly, as if only for Gerry and me to hear though he looked at neither of us: "Everybody hated her."

"I didn't," I said.

"It was either her or me," he said, and was to repeat a number of times that afternoon, as though to impress it on us. Neither of us responded.

"She made me professional," he complained at some point, his fury softening a little into bitterness.

I had read and heard about an English preference for amateur status in the arts, in any field of study and every kind of sport. An Englishman did what he did for the love of it; Americans wrote to sell their work, their culture being so much more materialistic. So the story ran. Americans might love writing poetry too, but that was not enough for them. It had not been enough for *her*; and by foisting her mercenary outlook on him, she had corrupted him. That, more or less, was what he was getting at. It was fiddle-faddle, of course. Hughes was delighted with having his work in print, published by the most prestigious house in the poetry business. His job as a presenter of poetry readings with the BBC was not a burdensome chore to him. For one thing, it spread his fame. If it were even partially true that he owed his growing reputation and commercial success to his wife for pressing him to sell his work, it was cause for gratitude, not resentment. I'd heard her say that to be a serious writer one "must be professional" about it and once I asked what she meant precisely. She replied that one's work should be submitted "correctly typed, with double spacing, on clean paper." I still have her list, neatly hand-written, of periodicals that

wrong. Or I didn't want to inflict hurt, which was equally cowardly. I wouldn't hesitate to say such a thing now.

I also wondered when he'd told her of his plan to return to her. Had it been on the Saturday night before her death? If so, it would raise new speculations about her moods and her decision. But I didn't ask him.

In another burst of speech he asked me if I'd read *The Bell Jar*. I told him I had. And did I know that it was autobiographical? I did. So I also knew that she'd tried to kill herself before they'd met? I did.

"It was *in* her, you see," he said. "But I told her that if she wrote about it profoundly enough, she would conquer it."

"And you don't think she wrote about it profoundly enough?"

"No."

His *no* was a sort of verbal shrug, implying: *obviously not—doesn't this funeral prove it?* He didn't care to know what I might think of it, and I didn't tell him, but in fact I agree with him. *The Bell Jar* is about an attempted suicide, but comes nowhere near to explaining it.

Later Hughes would say, and publish, that despite what happened, he believed Sylvia had had a great capacity for happiness. He could be right. She might have been happy, given a faithful husband, six children, more domestic help, more money, more acclaim, and ever-continuing luck. But, but . . . : children are hostages to fortune; the male sex-drive is always on the watch for opportunity; and if luck keeps children safe and well and husband home, there is always whatever it is that gnaws at one's own heart. She was a depressive, and sooner or later could have come to feel that, just as kindness is inadequate, and beauty hard to bear, happiness itself can be intolerable.

4

Afterward

Hughes was faithful to the poems. Very soon after her death he saw to their publication, although they made such bitter accusations against him. Quickly her fame began to spread. Within a week or two a journalist from *Time* magazine came to see me to ask about Sylvia's last days. The editor, she said, was "touched by the story of Sylvia Plath." As that story appeared in *Time,* her suicide came when it did because the friends she had been staying with "let her go too soon." She made no suggestion—nor did the others who repeated it in years to come—as to what we should have done to keep her.

I did not then and do not now believe that anything we could have done or said would have kept Sylvia from her suicide, since we had nothing to do with its causes. Perhaps we delayed it for a few days, during which the children were cared for, Sylvia had company and enjoyed some good meals. She needed the shelter of our warm, comfortable house, with music and books in it, where children's needs were catered for, and where she was always welcomed and listened to. Could I or Gerry or anyone at all have given her a reason for living if her children were not reason enough?

I've even thought it possible that she lost her passion for poetry. Some of those last poems of hers with their doggerel rhythms suggest to me that she was stamping on the grave of poetry itself. It's not an absurd idea if writing made her feel worse. The thing one makes must be worth what it takes. Was it in her case? Millions of her readers would answer yes. I think she would have been surprised by her mother's answer to that question, which she asked and answered as we walked along the Thames embankment on a warm night, the summer after Sylvia's death. It was no.

From the moment Dr. Horder told me she was dead, any trace of guilt that might have troubled me the night before vanished. I felt many emotions—so many chased each other that oddly enough it was very like feeling none at all—but guilt was not one of them. Horror, loss, pity, grief, all came and went and came again, and hurt and anger too because she left not a word for us.

I tried to suppress the anger. If I showed it to others I always said it was over her abandonment of her children. That was righteous anger. But it was not righteous or reasonable to feel that she owed me, or us, gratitude, explanation, or farewell. Mere social graces! Should they matter to one who was overwhelmed by despair? Why should she, *in extremis*, think of us, who had after all not affected the drama of her life to any important extent? I was a bit-player, one who had done to swell a scene or two. Stars though we all are, each in his own life, to one another we are just "someone else." To this effect I lectured myself.

Though both Gerry and I felt she had discarded us along with the whole intolerable world, we made every allowance for her. But now I don't. Now I say that I did not deserve to be contemned by her. Other friends deserted her, men she courted in her loneliness spurned her, publishers refused her novel, the editors of the *New Yorker* rejected poems of hers on the grounds that they couldn't understand them. But I had neither rejected nor hurt her. As a would-be poet, I deserved to be humbled by her talent; but I myself did not deserve to be humiliated by her disdain.

She left no last-minute scribbled note to Hughes, but she left him her poetry, knowing that he would understand those last poems as suicide notes, not apologetic but accusatory. Her death itself was addressed to him, and through him to the world. Nothing was addressed to me. Did she perhaps think that my appreciation of her poetry would make me feel I'd received a legacy from her along with everybody else? I doubt she thought of me at all. But she did, I believe, think of posterity. She probably saw that she could accomplish recognition as a contributor to English literature better by dying than living—once the poems were written and neatly typed on clean paper, and that was done before she came to us. Fame was her last desire, as it had been her first. Her *Letters Home* are letters to Posterity as are Hughes's *Birthday Letters*.

Neither Gerry nor I expected that Sylvia's eruption into our existence and her violent exit from it would have any lasting or significant bearing on the course of our own lives. But it did. At least it had direct bearing on mine, and so inevitably on Gerry's.

To mention only the effects of which I was most conscious at the time, it changed my tastes and my choice of companions. Or it helped to change them. I'd had an addiction to poetry, and my growing out of it was at least partly assisted by my painful involvement in the lives of these poets. Now I have no patience with poets, romantics, or aesthetes of any stripe.

After I'd read *Ariel, Crossing the Water,* and *Winter Trees,* I didn't read anything of Sylvia's for the next thirty-nine years. I stopped buying poetry, and read it less and less. I bought but did not read the *Journals.* I did not buy *Letters Home.* For years I tried not to think or talk about Sylvia. When books about her came out I read any reviews I happed upon, but never the books themselves. They sounded silly most of them, some preposterous, none interesting.

In 1973 a woman from Boston found me and asked me to tell her what I remembered about Sylvia's last days so she could put it into a short biography for the New York feminist periodical, *Ms.* I asked her what she had found out, and when I heard how wrong it was, I couldn't resist the temptation to put her right. She returned to America, and for a time, as more questions occurred to her, we corresponded. I sent her a copy of the autopsy that Mr. Goodchild brought me. When I went to New York to see my publishers about a book I was writing on another subject, I took a bus to Boston, and the would-be biographer and I talked about Sylvia again. On my return to London I wrote to her once more, but received no answer.

In 1988 Hughes's sister Olwyn introduced me to Anne Stevenson, the Plath biographer semiauthorized by Hughes. When, in Olwyn's presence, I told Stevenson what Hughes had said at Sylvia's funeral—that "everybody hated her"—Olwyn stopped me. Loyalty to her brother made her a fierce censor. "You can't put that in," she shot at Stevenson. In the end, nothing that I related about the funeral appeared in Stevenson's book *Bitter Fame,* the text of which was approved by Olwyn. It does, however, carry Dido Merwin's dying testimony that Sylvia was to blame for Hughes's infidelity and the breakdown of their marriage.

Dido Merwin had been married to the American poet W. S. Merwin. One night in the winter of 1988–1989, after she and I and Olwyn had dined together at a Chinese restaurant, she asked me if she could talk to me alone. I drove her back to a house where she was lodging in St. John's Wood. Because everyone in the house had gone to bed, she couldn't, she said, ask me in. So we sat in the car for two or three hours while she told me what she "really" wanted to say about Sylvia and Ted. She was incurably ill, and wanted to tell her story to someone in case she died before she could write it down. She thought I was the right person to tell it to, but I was too cold and sleepy to take much of it in. Fortunately for her, she did in fact live long enough to record it herself. The only certainty I took away with me from her long, emotional narration was that she "hated Sylvia and loved Ted," whom she regarded as a poet almost equal in stature to her husband Bill.

In 1992 or thereabouts Janet Malcolm, a writer for the *New Yorker*, tracked me down and came to tea. She was of the psychoanalytical persuasion, and was interested in why people who talked about Sylvia talked about her as they did. I was interested in why that interested her, and thought the answer might have something to do with the questions she asked. Meeting with her was like standing in a room lined with distorting mirrors. I must have disappointed her. She made no use of anything I said.

In 1999 Hughes published *Birthday Letters*. A review drew my attention to a poem in it called

Dreamers. It is about Assia, on the "fatal day" she visited Court Green; the day she "picked her way among the cowpats in her high-heeled shoes;" the day Hughes began seriously to lust after her; the day when Sylvia's ideal life began to unravel. In it Hughes blames Assia for what happened, Sylvia next, himself not at all, but then again it was not really the fault of any of them, but of Fate, in whose hand all three were but helpless tools.

Fate was a big theme with both Hughes and Sylvia. I knew they were fascinated by occultism. A witch lived near them in Devon, Sylvia assured me. She and Hughes used a planchette to receive messages from the spirit world. Hughes believed he had mystical foresight, and even a degree of personal command over the future. At first I'd thought she regarded all this as something of a joke, but came to realize she was serious. Both of them believed that doing violence to reason released intuitive creativeness.

5

Slightly Filthy

Dreamers is sickeningly anti-Semitic. (And what, I wonder, makes it "a poem?") Some of its vocabulary could have come spitting out of an issue of the *Völkischer Beobachter*, the organ of the Nazi party: "greasy" (was Assia's speech); "filthy" (she was, though only "slightly"); "death-camp" closely followed by "soot" ("soot-softness"), "her Jewishness"; "this Lilith of abortions," a "creature" who *touches the hair of your children / With tiger-painted nails*—a suggestion of child-victimization. The gold by means of which Jews are said by anti-Semites to plot, century in and century out, to take over the world is not mentioned, but "Kensington jeweller" is, with scorn ("her Kensington jeweller's elocution"). Some of the ideas could have dripped from a medieval text on witchcraft: *She sniffed us out; watching you, through smoke, / Her black-ringed grey iris, slightly unnatural, / Was Black Forest wolf, a witch's daughter.* And there are notions that could be found in either of those enchiridions on the doctrinal use of terror and fire: *The Fate she carried / Sniffed us out / And assembled us, inert ingredients / For its experiment,* a hint of both Dr. Mengele and the ancient blood-libel.

Hysteria underlies the self-assurance of the lines. In its heat, the Nazis and their victims are alchemized into one: *Hitler's mutilations / Kept you company, weeding the onions; An ex-Nazi*

Youth Sabra; A German / Russian Israeli with the gaze of a demon. All of which is a jumble of rubbish. Only the sons and daughters of a Jewish mother (and converts) are recognized by Jews to be Jewish, and as her mother was not, Assia was not. Nor was she a Sabra, a name (meaning prickly-pear) applied to Jews born in the Holy Land. Assia was taken there as a child, before the State of Israel existed. She was Canadian, and even though German-born could not have been a member of the Hitler Youth, the Nazi organization for boys. As her Jewish father must have taken his family out of Germany before 1939, she would hardly have been old enough to join the *Bund Deutscher Mädel* (League of German Maidens) or the *Kraft durch Freude* (Strength through Joy) girls' movement; and in any case would have been ineligible for either, her father being a Jew.

Hughes's technique seems to have been to bang down words in the hope that their connotations would convey an emotional impression

of a subject, in this case a woman's dangerous-
ness and disgustingness. He must have meant
the reader to be awed and appalled that with
this slightly filthy demonic creature—who was
also "beautiful"—he fell in love.

It was love of Evil itself. Lilith, the first wife
of Adam and the serpent in Eden, is the very
spirit of Evil. I think he did fall in love with it,
but years before he met Assia. His works tell us
that. It's why they have wide appeal in our
Gnostic New Age. It's why critics lauded his
"admirable violence."

I have heard two defenses of *Dreamers*; one
of the poet for writing it, the other of the poem
itself.

The defense of the poet is to be found in an
interview Hughes granted in November 1998 to
a journalist with the distinctly Israeli name
of Eilat Negev. Between him and Hughes an
emotional explanation was concocted which
Hughes must have hoped would vindicate him-

self and justify the poem. This (presumably) Jewish journalist declared: "For Assia Wevill— the threat of the Holocaust was a real and experienced terror." Nonsense! German Jews who were old enough to know what was going on in the 1930s had reason to fear the Nazis, but the Holocaust was beyond even their greatest fears. Assia had been a child then, and was borne off to safety in Canada. Still, out of this imagined terror that by implication enriched the interest and pathos of Assia's emotional *Bildung*, Negev constructs, with the poet's help, a link between her and Hughes of a world-historical kind, making what was a sordid love affair and cruel betrayal into an event worthy of Fate's attention: "Hughes too had experienced an upbringing under the shadow of death."

Indeed? How?

"He was born . . . in 1930 in a small Yorkshire village, many of whose menfolk had perished during the First World War. At Gallipoli, his father was one of only seventeen survivors of a whole regiment, and his unspoken pain was felt by his son."

Unspoken?

" 'I am like a second-generation Holocaust survivor,' [Hughes said] 'whose father kept silent about the horrors he's been in.' "

Kept silent? Then how . . . ?

" 'I heard a lot from my uncles, who fought with him.' " And were also among the seventeen survivors? A family blessed!

Hughes goes on to speak of his shaman-like magic powers, and to claim that his poetry is curative. So his writing of *Dreamers* was, one must infer, a duty of his holy office. But for whom was it balm or therapy? Since Assia and Sylvia were beyond healing, the patient must have been himself. Can one blame a man racked by vicarious suffering for resorting to any remedy, even one that is poisonous to others? Yes, one can and I do. Hughes's self-exoneration is not merely pretentious twaddle, it is blasphemy—if the word can be used in a secular sense, and I think it can. To pose as a victim at the expense of millions of real victims, is to sin against humankind. With this special pleading to a Jewish reporter, who was apparently insensitive to pretension, this poet of weighty reputation reveals a weak-minded insouciance. As a defense it falls flat.

The other defense, of the poem itself, is that it is not entirely an expression of Hughes's own thoughts, but that the revulsion and scorn in it are to be understood as Sylvia's, to whom the poem is addressed: "She fascinated you"; "she shocked you"; "you saw . . . "; "you cultivated her"; "you were astonished, maybe envious," "I refused to interpret."

I don't believe she thought or spoke the ugly anti-Semitisms of *Dreamers*. It is Hughes's choice of words, his psychology on display. She was not anti-Semitic; he was.

In some of her last poems she claims an empathetic understanding of the Jews confined in the Nazi camps and killed in the gas ovens. From *Daddy*: *Chuffing me off like a Jew. / A Jew to Dachau, Auschwitz, Belsen. / I began to talk like a Jew. I think I may well be a Jew.* And from *Lady Lazarus: So, so, Herr Doktor. / So, Herr Enemy. . . . / Ash, ash—/ You poke and stir. / Flesh, bone, there is nothing there—/ A cake of soap, / A wedding ring, / A gold filling.*

It has been suggested to me that part of her reason for "identifying herself" with the Jewish victims of the Holocaust was a fear of having it said that anti-Semitism underlay her hatred of Assia. I don't think so; she had enough reason to hate Assia. I have been asked whether she turned to Gerry and me for friendship because of our being Jewish, and I doubt that too. Nothing she ever said suggested it. And the relationship doesn't need accounting for; it flourished in its season.

Yet, when all that is said—I do find cause to be cautious in my defense of her. The claim to empathy goes, I think, too far. And then there is this: *The Sunday lamb cracks in its fat. . . . / The same fire/ Melting the tallow heretics, / Ousting the Jews. . . . / They do not die. . . . / The ovens glowed like heavens, incandescent. / It is a heart, / This holocaust I walk in, / O golden child the world will kill and eat.* The poem is titled *Mary's Song.* Irresistibly now it brings to my mind the attempt by an order of nuns to turn Auschwitz into a Catholic shrine. Of course, I argue with myself, Sylvia meant no harm by her bit of syncretism. She just hadn't thought her idea through very well; or she lacked some knowledge she should have had.

Very well. But then again there is this, in *Letters Home* (October 21, 1962):

"What the person out of Belsen—physical or psychological—wants is nobody saying the birdies still go tweet-tweet, but the full knowledge that somebody else has been there and knows the *worst*, just what it is like." (Her italics)

It provokes me to speak directly to her, to say reproachfully, as if to give her a chance to reword an utterance that came out wrongly: "Now come on, Sylvia! Do you seriously believe your poems could do that? Do you really think they would be of use to 'a person out of Belsen'? That they would convey to a survivor of a Nazi concentration camp that you had 'been there' and knew 'the *worst*, just what it was like?'"

Her biographer Anne Stevenson believed her, and went even further, making a claim that surpassed Sylvia's own. Writing in *Poetry Review* (Winter 1988/89) Stevenson glibly asserted: "Her suffering was indeed *on a scale* to compare with the Holocaust—*all the more terrible* because it was self-inflicted and lacked a physical dimension." (My italics)

I tell myself that Sylvia would have recognized this for what it is—stupid. And I still maintain that Sylvia was not anti-Semitic. But she should not have tried to dramatize her own unhappiness with such a comparison. It was enough that she was forsaken, rejected, burdened with children she could not cope with however much she loved them. She did not need a grander, more compelling explanation. It has a hollow ring. Rather than conveying her pain as more impressively extreme, it lessens it by making one wonder why she needed to exaggerate. The exaggeration taken with her suicide makes it all too probable that her final act was, like her "letters home," dedicated to Posterity. Too much the writer and too little the mother, did she gas herself because the story she invented for her life demanded that ending?

6

Myth

What she could not have foreseen was that her myth would be hijacked by the Feminist Movement, as it has been. She herself was no feminist; not, anyway, if feminism means scorning the traditional woman's role of wife and mother, homemaker and housekeeper. And I'm sure that although she raged against her dead father and faithless husband—the one for having died and been German, the other for being faithless and as brutal as a Nazi—she did not hate men in general. Far from it.

If feminists can savour an irony, here is one for them. I remember her looking up from reading something of mine to repeat a word she'd found in it. "Gynocratic," she said. "You've taught me a new word." (It didn't put her in my debt—she taught me more than one.) It was hardly imaginable then, in 1962, that a gynocratic age was about to descend on the Western World, and had anyone prophesied it and told her that she would be one of its icons, I think she'd have been surprised and possibly annoyed.

Perhaps the myth of Sylvia Plath the Feminist will fade away as intellectual fashions change. But another myth has been growing since Hughes died in 1999, or perhaps since he published his *Birthday Letters*. It is the Ted Hughes–Sylvia Plath myth, of two great poets locked together in a Wagnerian clinch that is at once an embrace of passionate love and an anguished struggle to the death. This is the myth they themselves indited. I don't like it any more than the other.

I want to reclaim for myself something of my friend Sylvia that she didn't spoil with her ambition. I find it in a thought she lends to the protective and loving mother of a newborn son in her radio play *Three Women*:

I do not will him to be exceptional,
It is the exception that interests the devil. . . .
I will him to be common,
To love me as I love him,
And to marry what he wants and where he will.